This Book Belongs To:

____

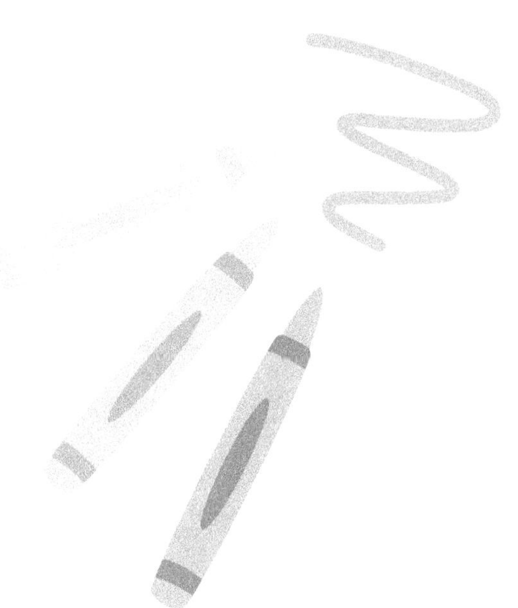

A a IS FOR

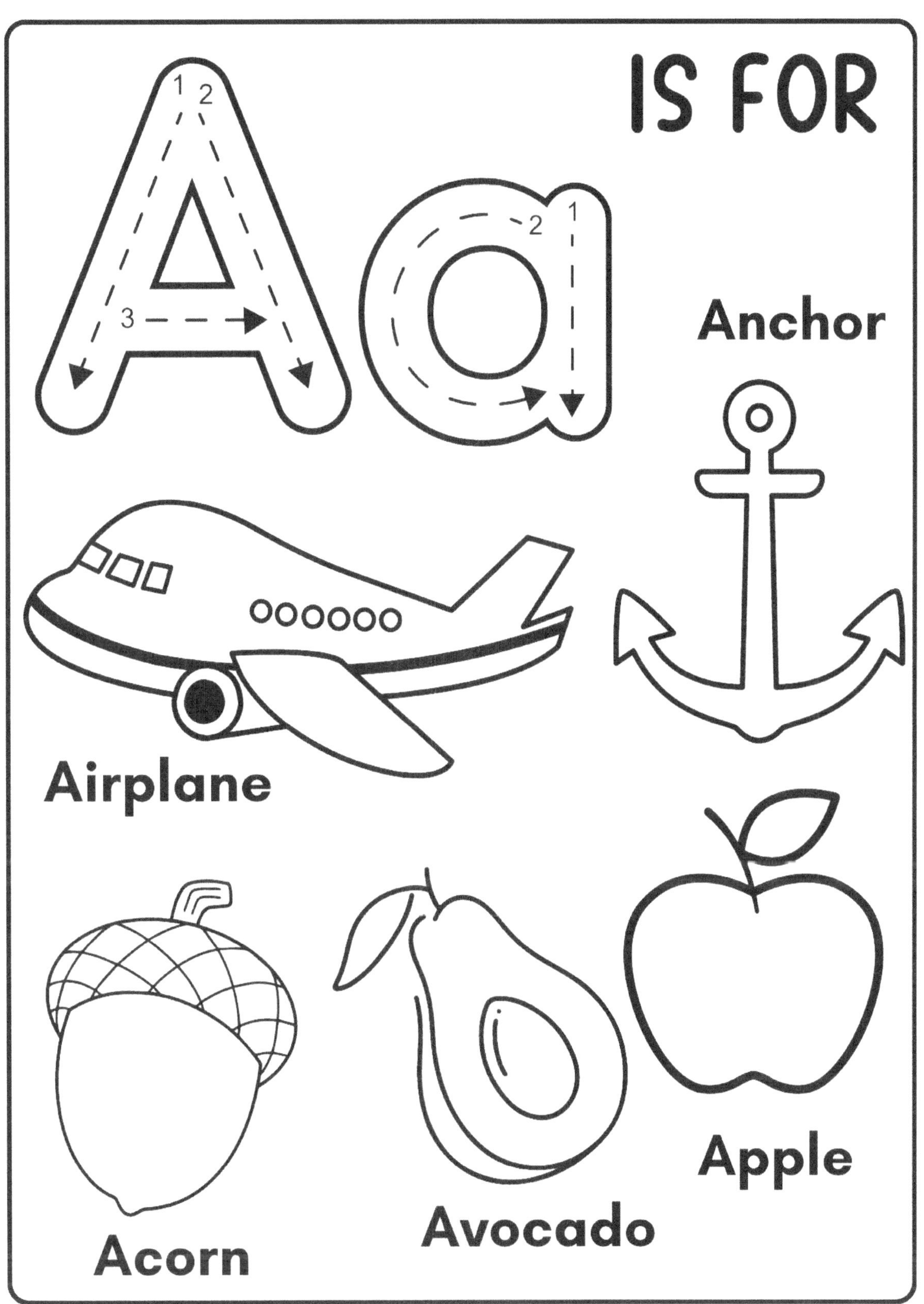

B b IS FOR

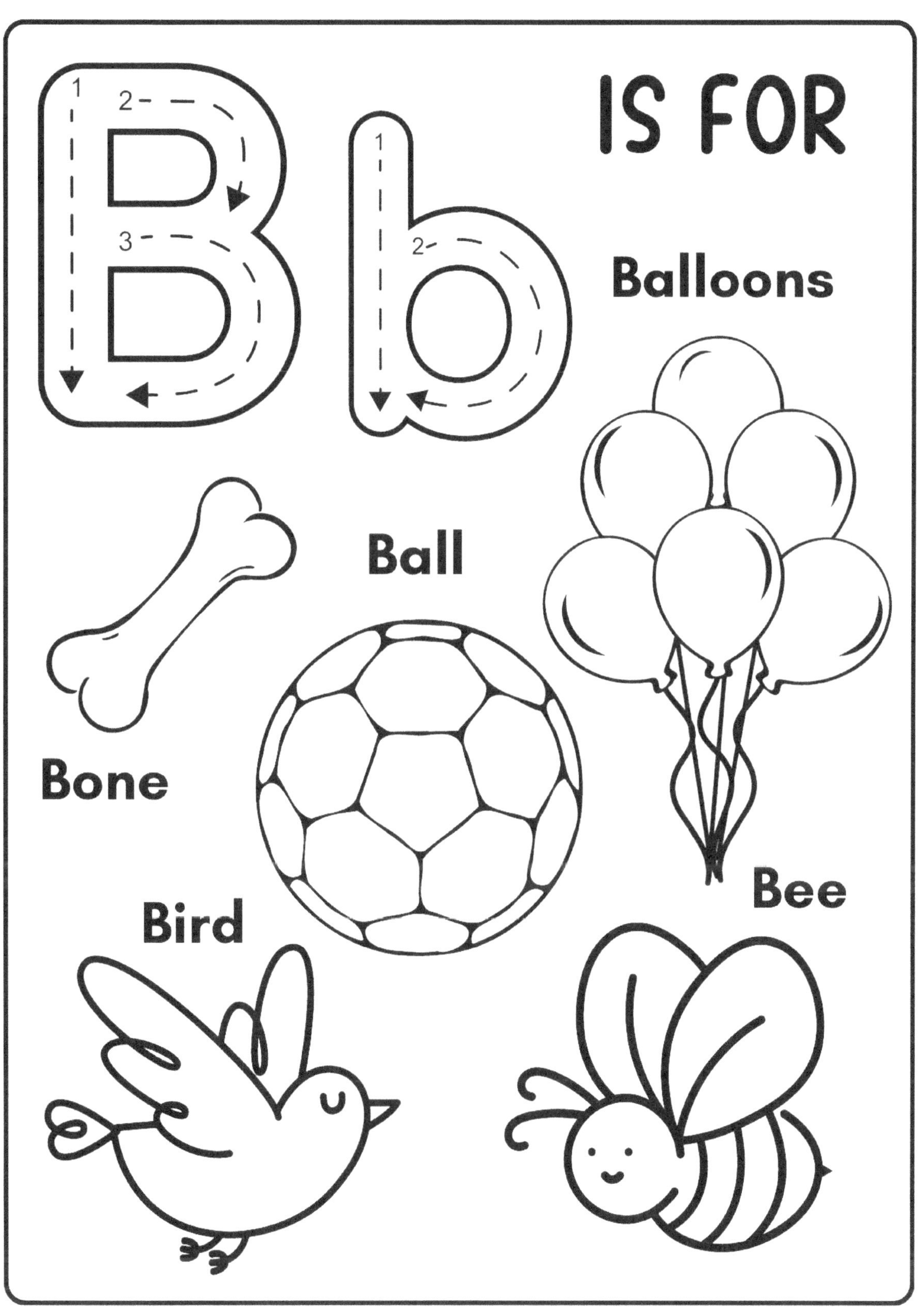

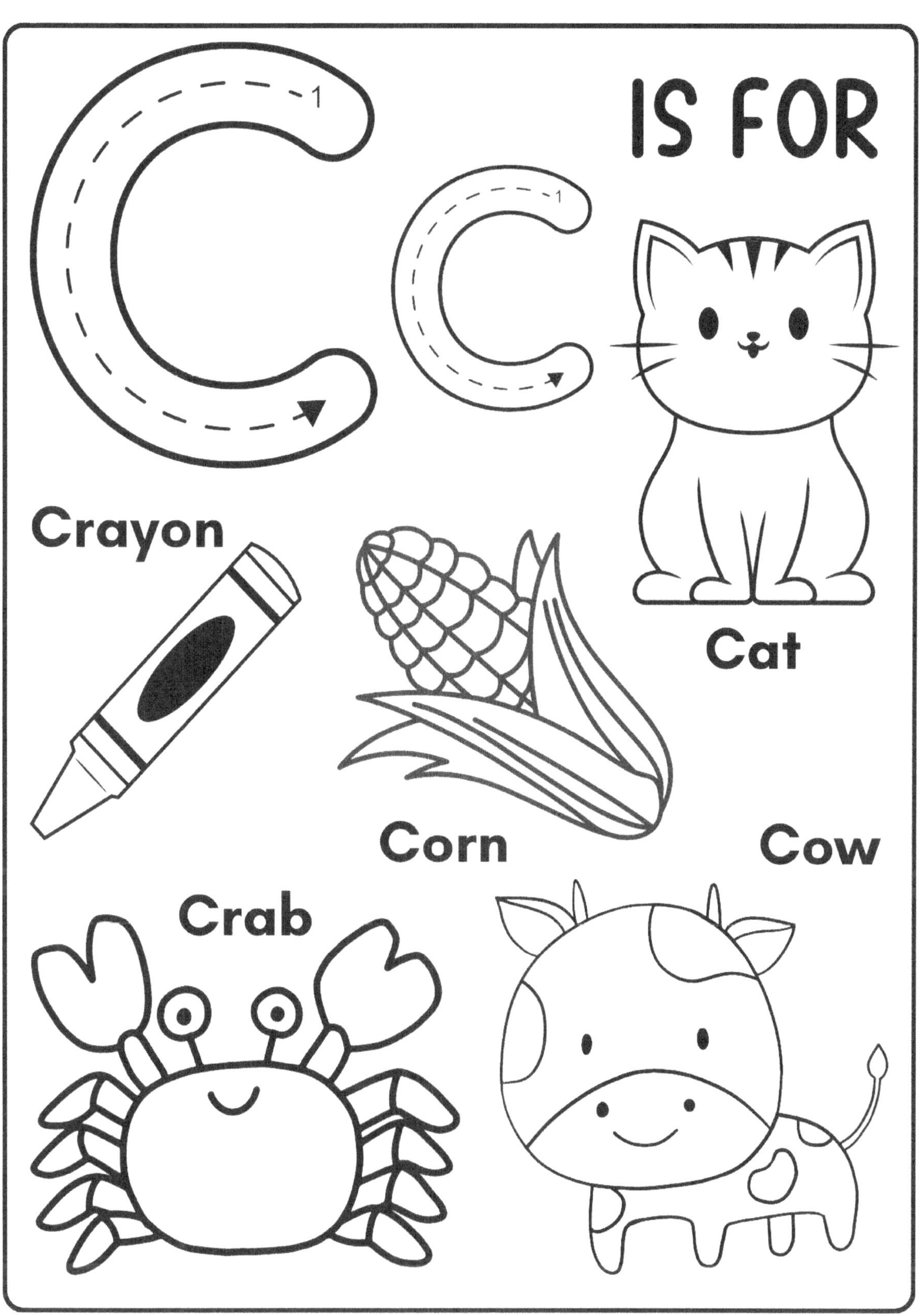

C c IS FOR
Crayon
Cat
Corn
Cow
Crab

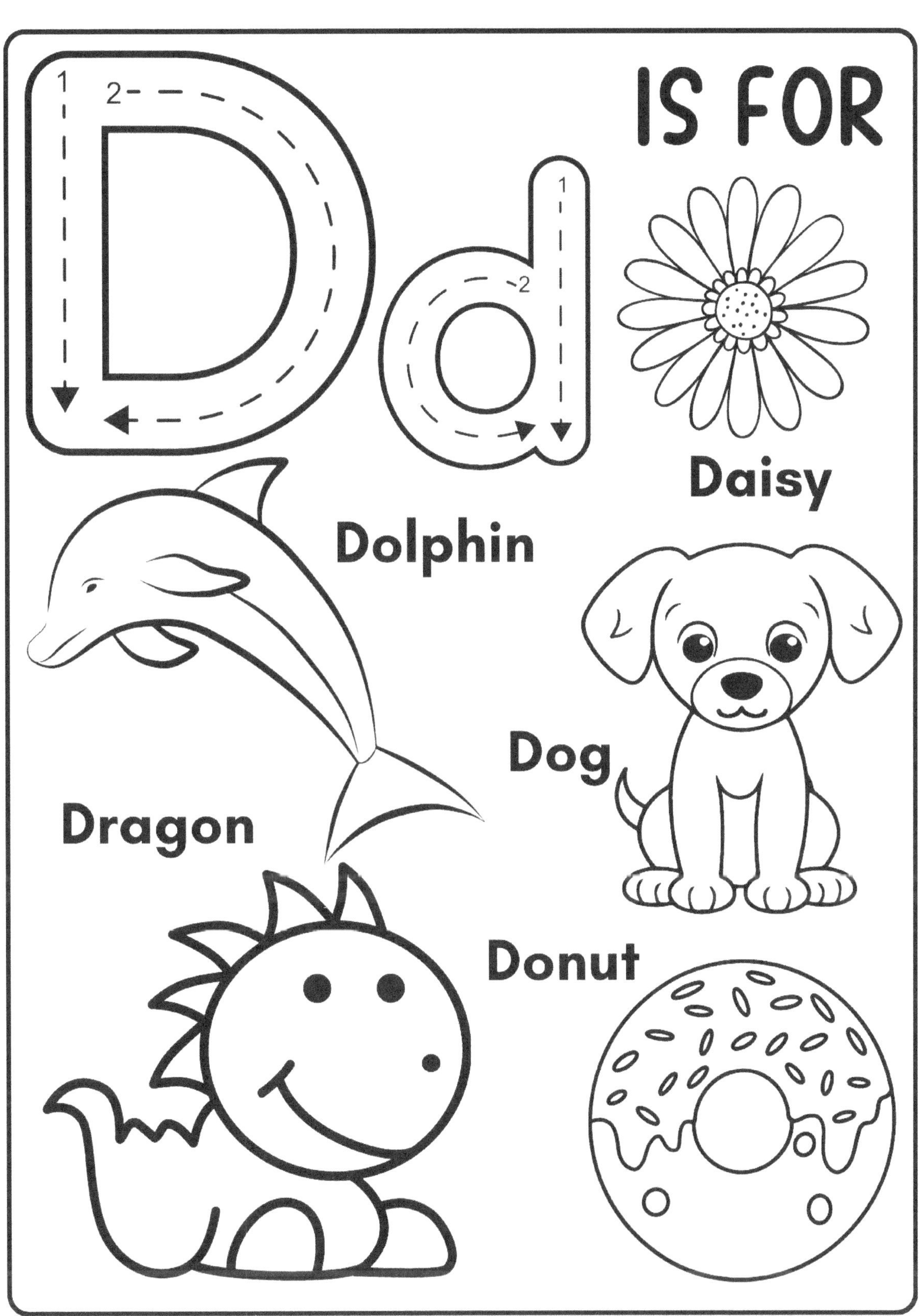

D d
IS FOR
Daisy
Dolphin
Dog
Dragon
Donut

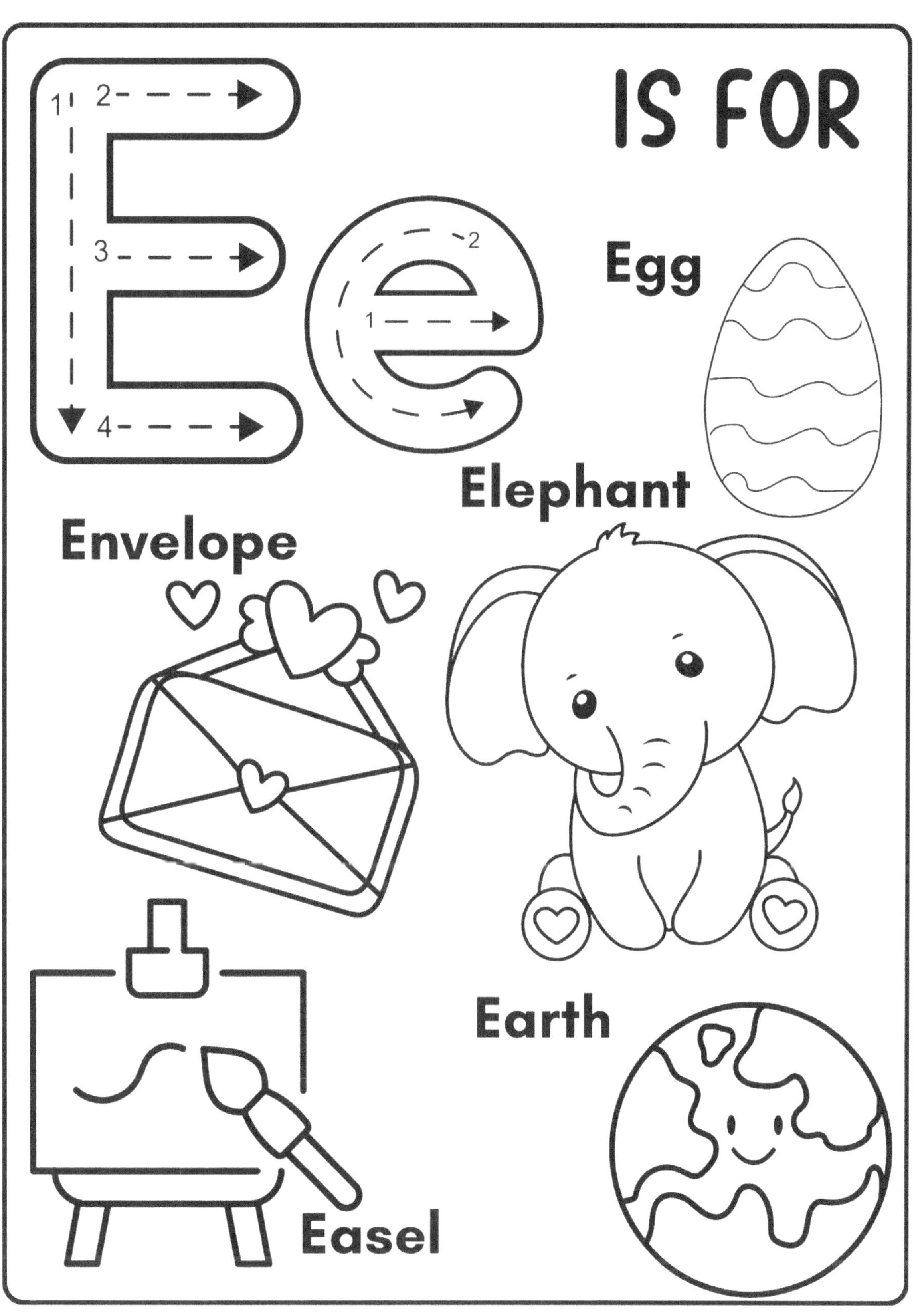

Ee
1 2 3 4 1 2
IS FOR
Egg
Elephant
Envelope
Earth
Easel

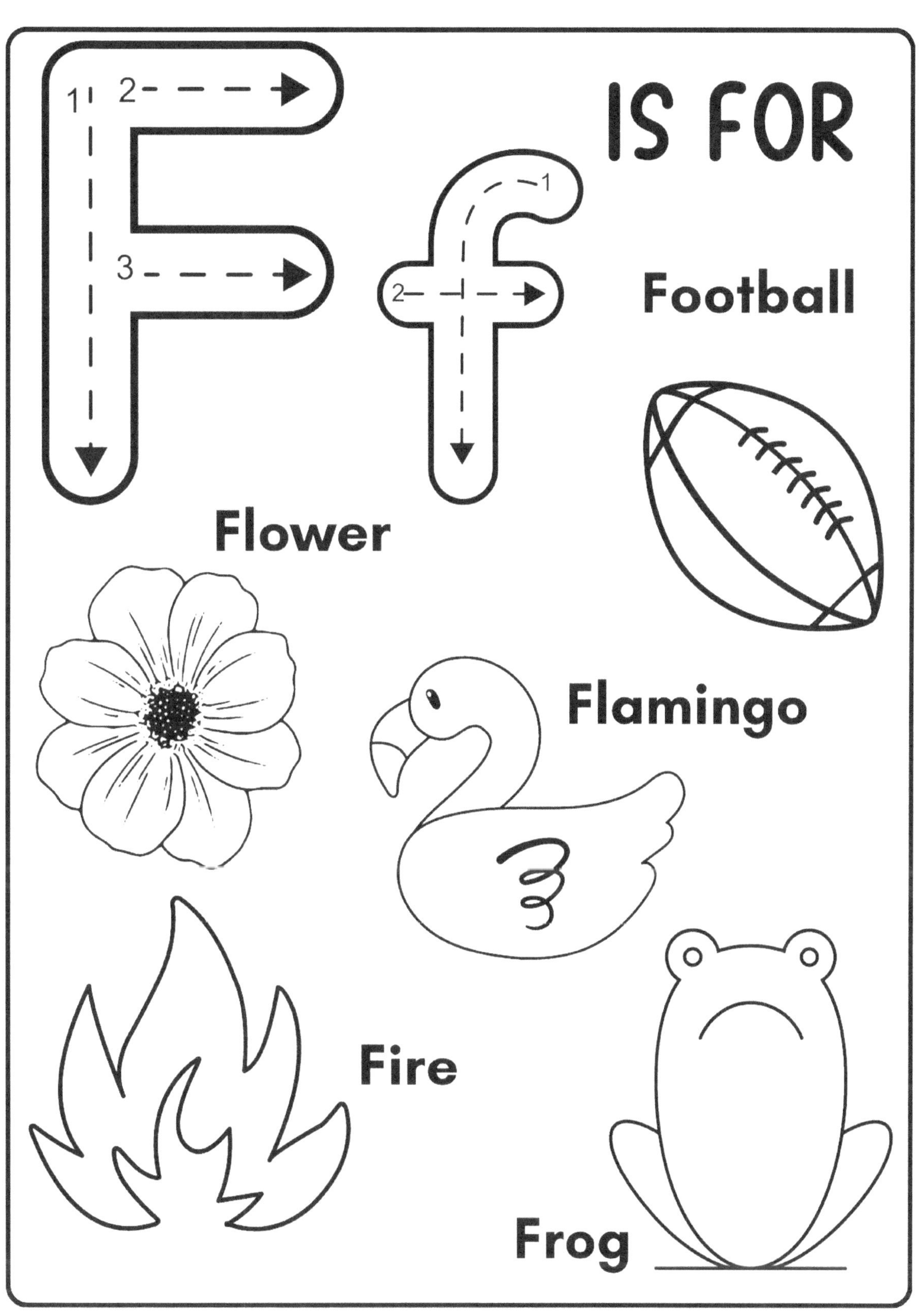

F
1 2 3
IS FOR
F f
1 2
Football
Flower
Flamingo
Fire
Frog

G g IS FOR

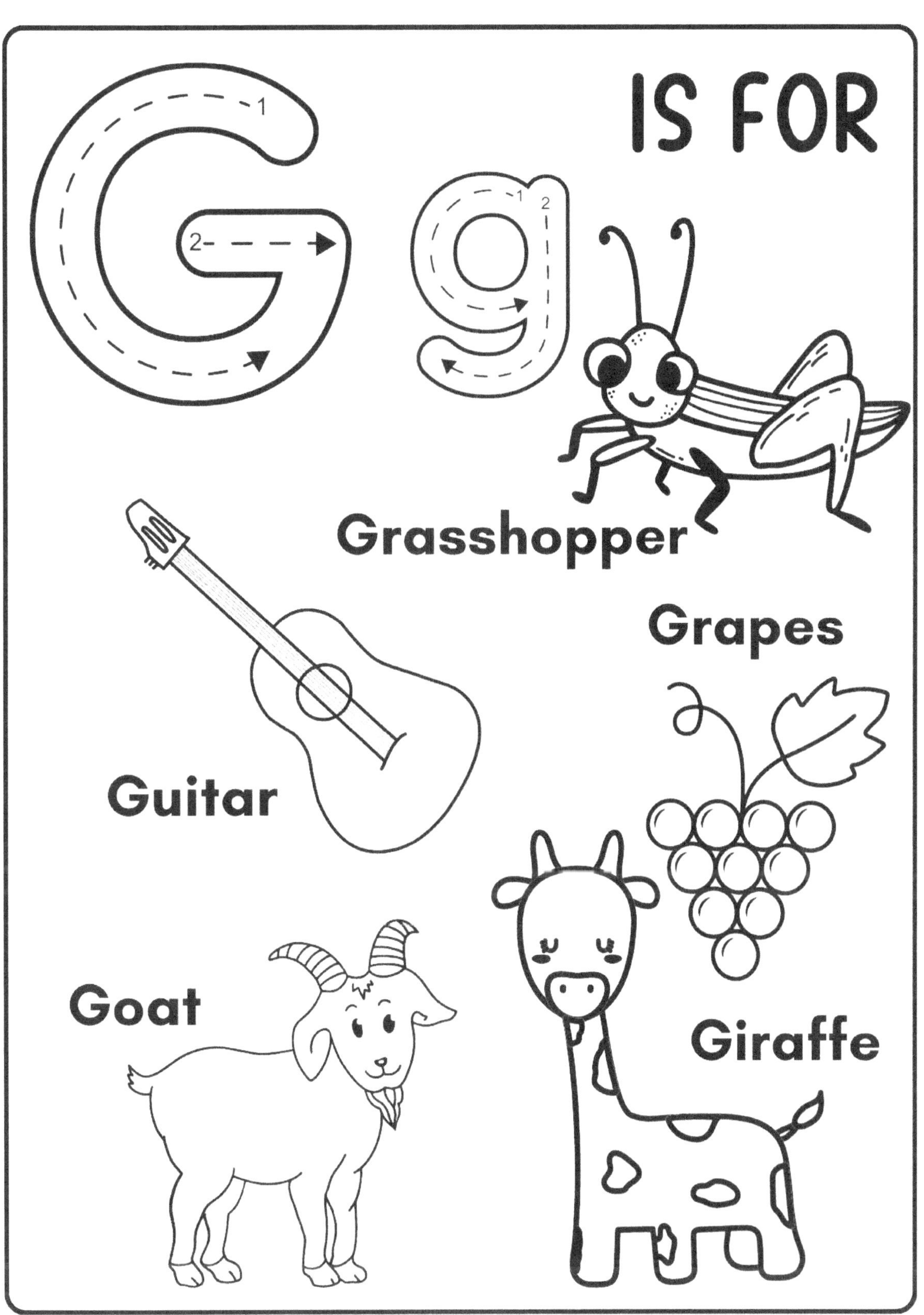

Hh

IS FOR

Hot Air Balloon

Hippo

Horse

Helicopter

Hamburger

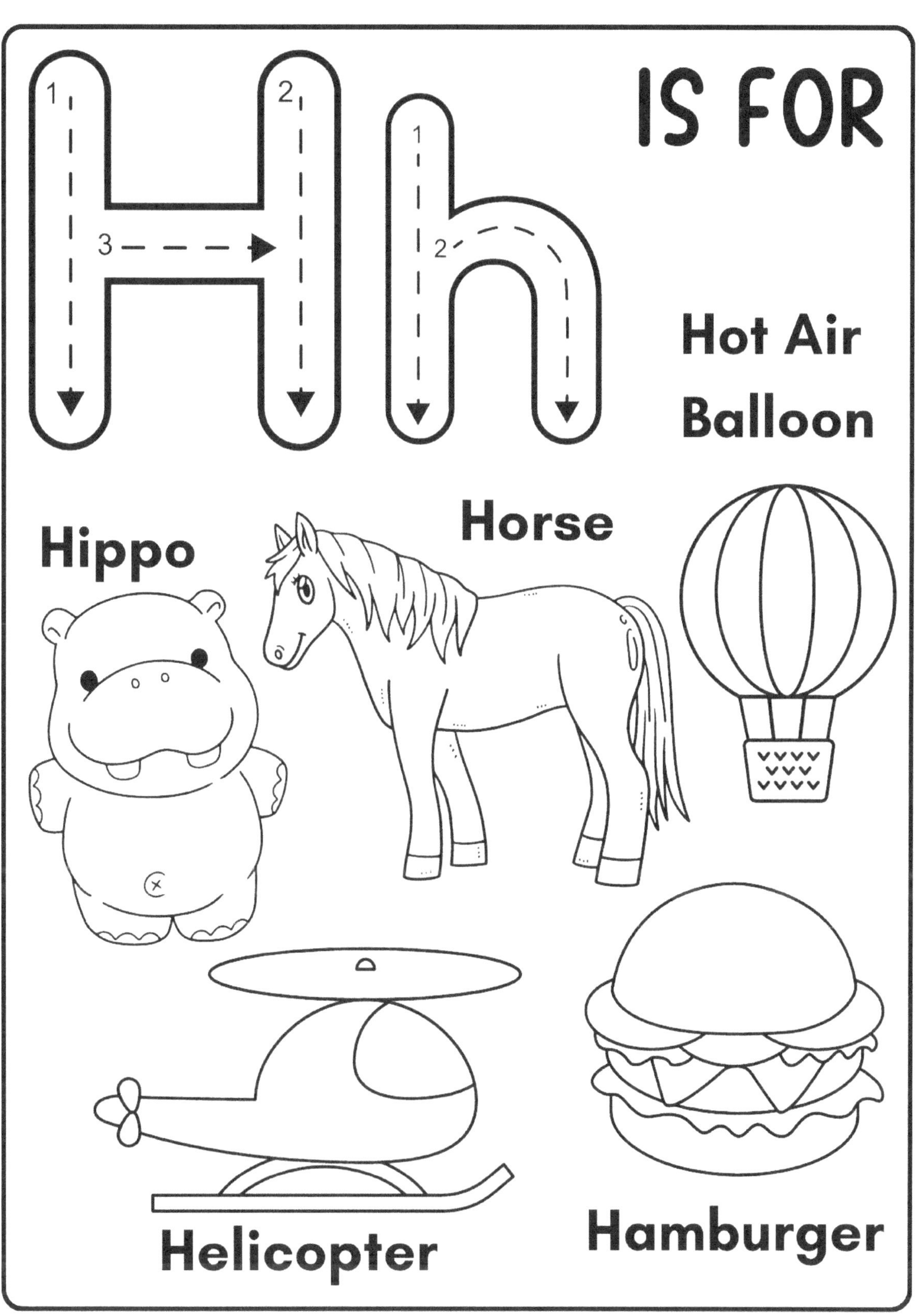

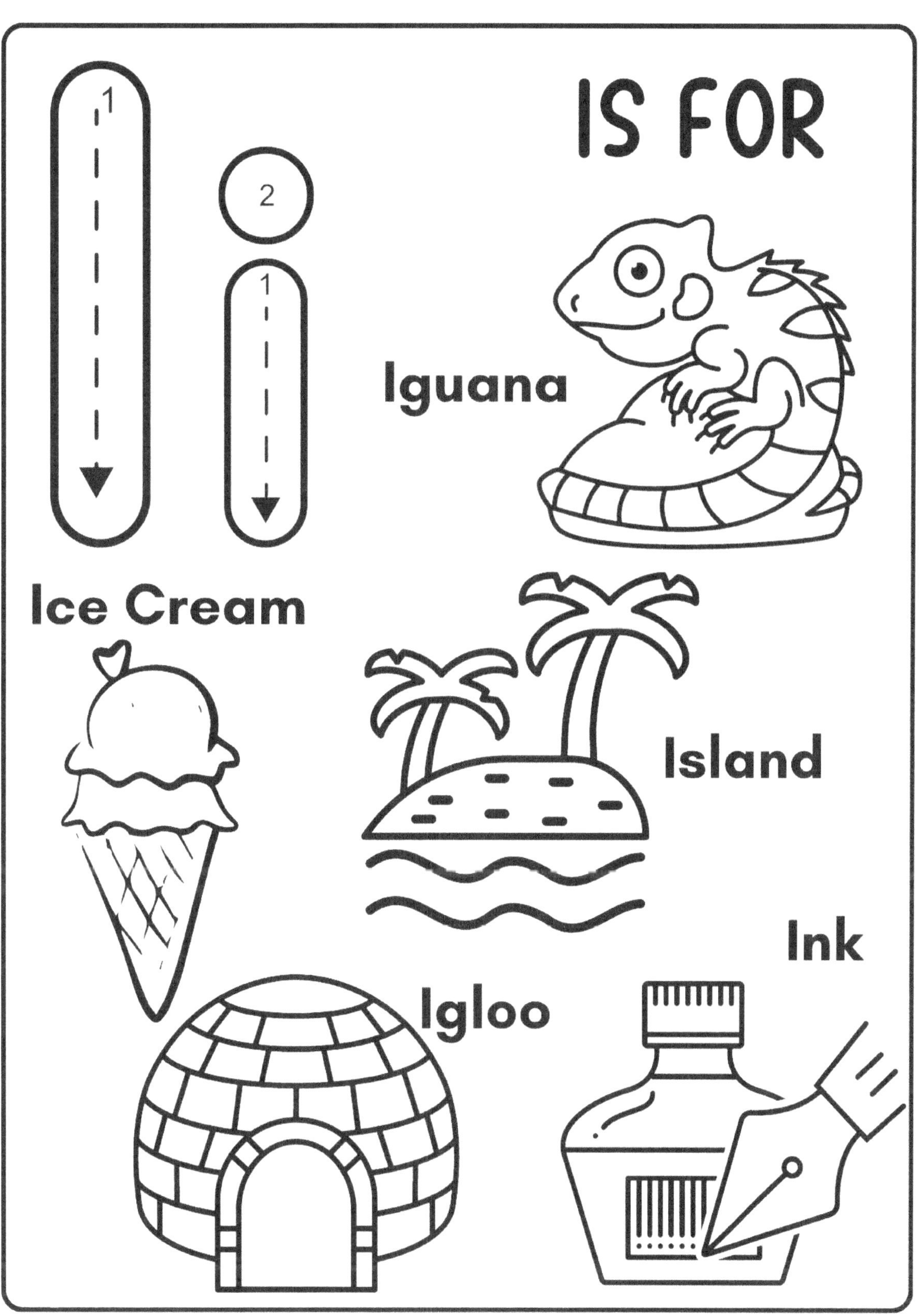

1
2
1
IS FOR
Iguana
Ice Cream
Island
Igloo
Ink

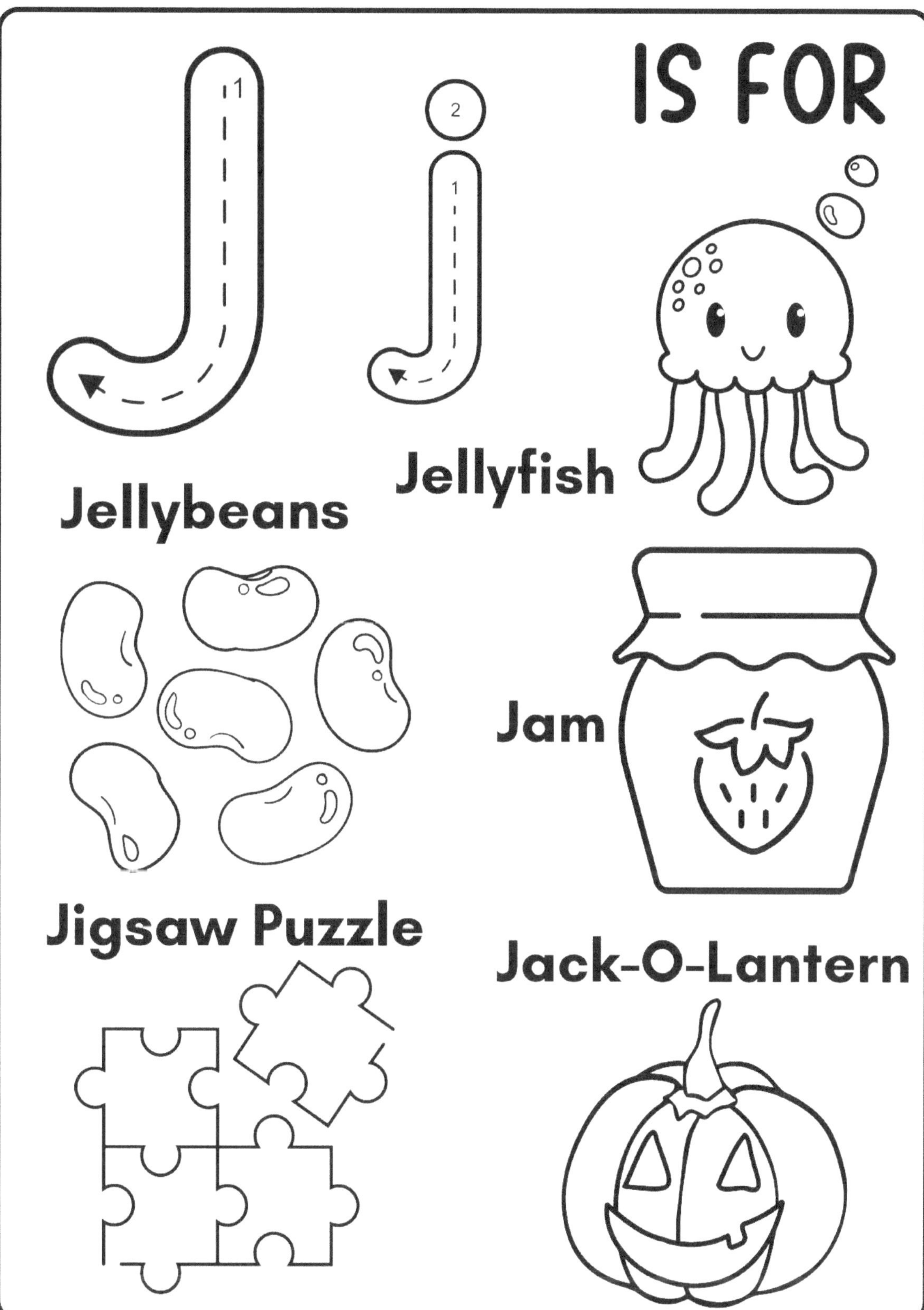

IS FOR
Jj
Jellybeans
Jellyfish
Jam
Jigsaw Puzzle
Jack-O-Lantern

K k IS FOR

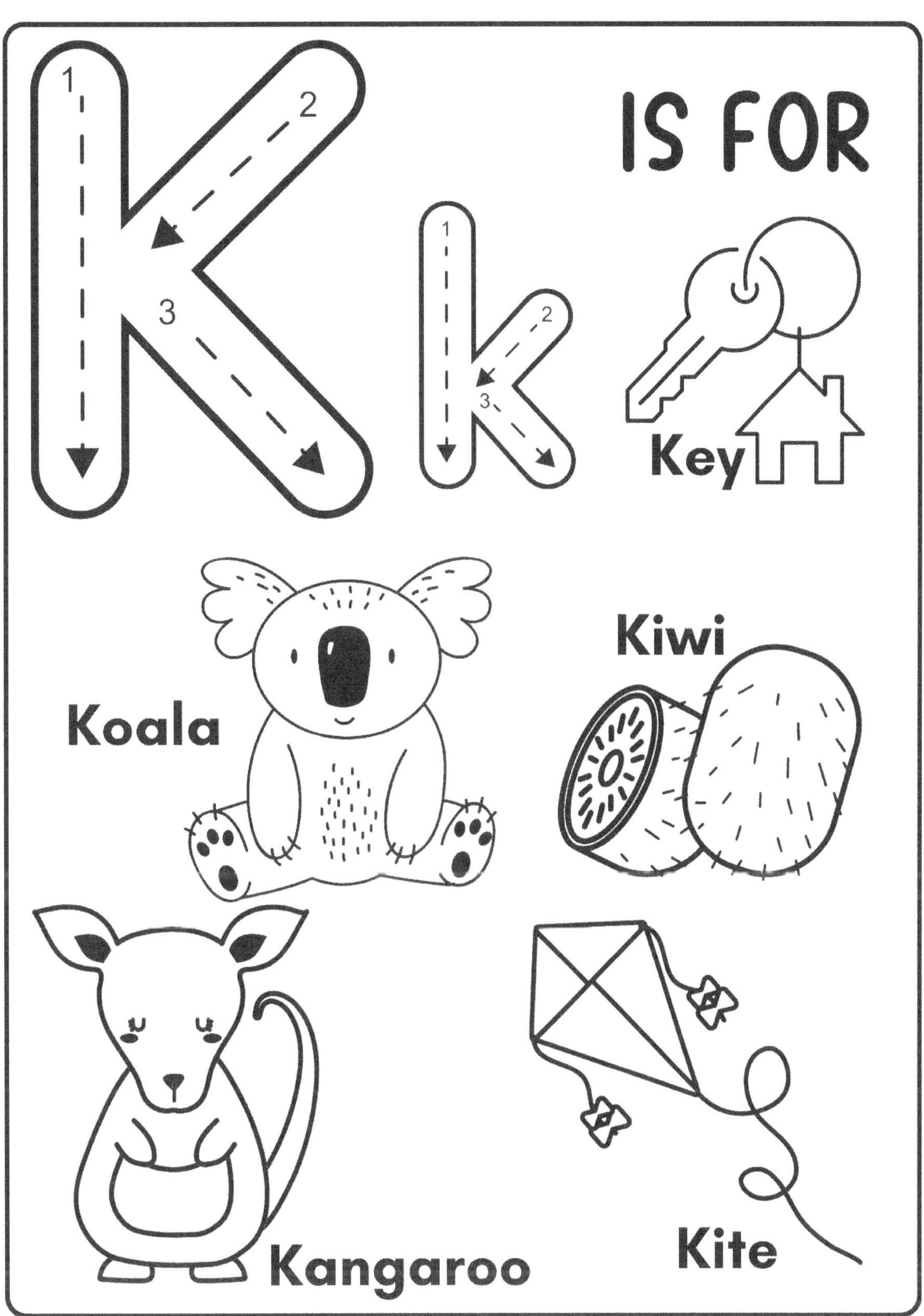

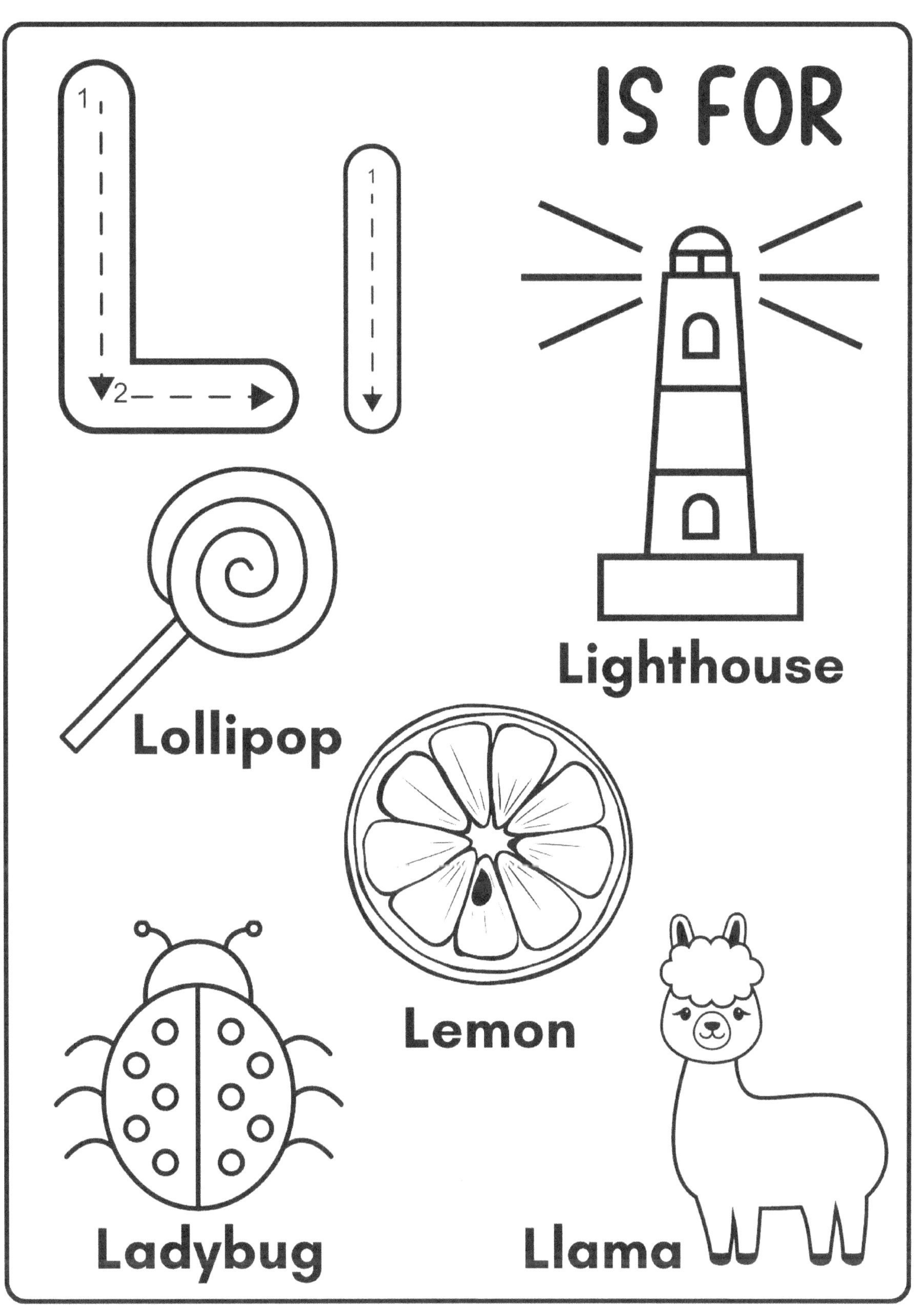

IS FOR
Lighthouse
Lollipop
Lemon
Ladybug
Llama

Mm IS FOR

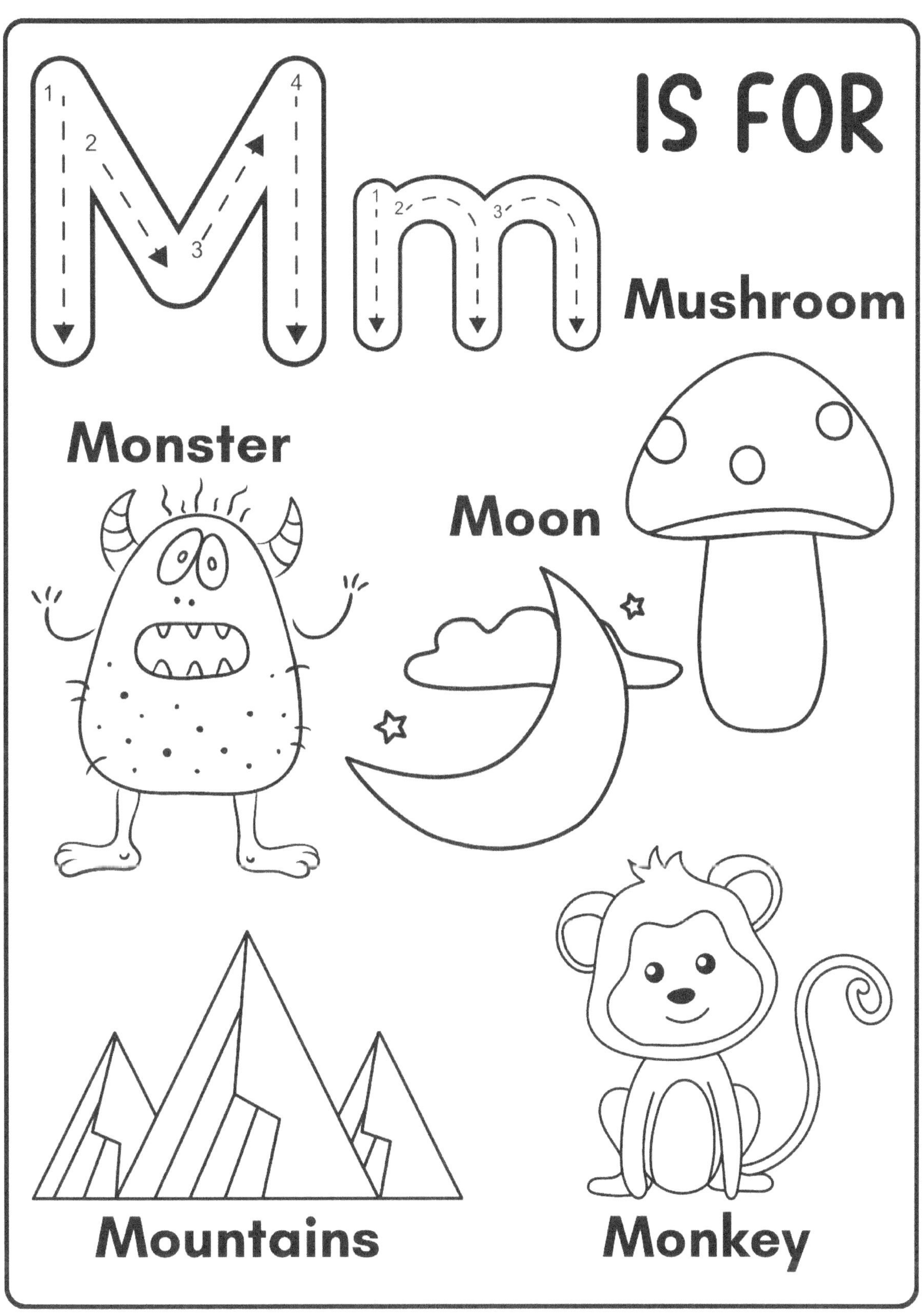

Mushroom

Monster

Moon

Mountains

Monkey

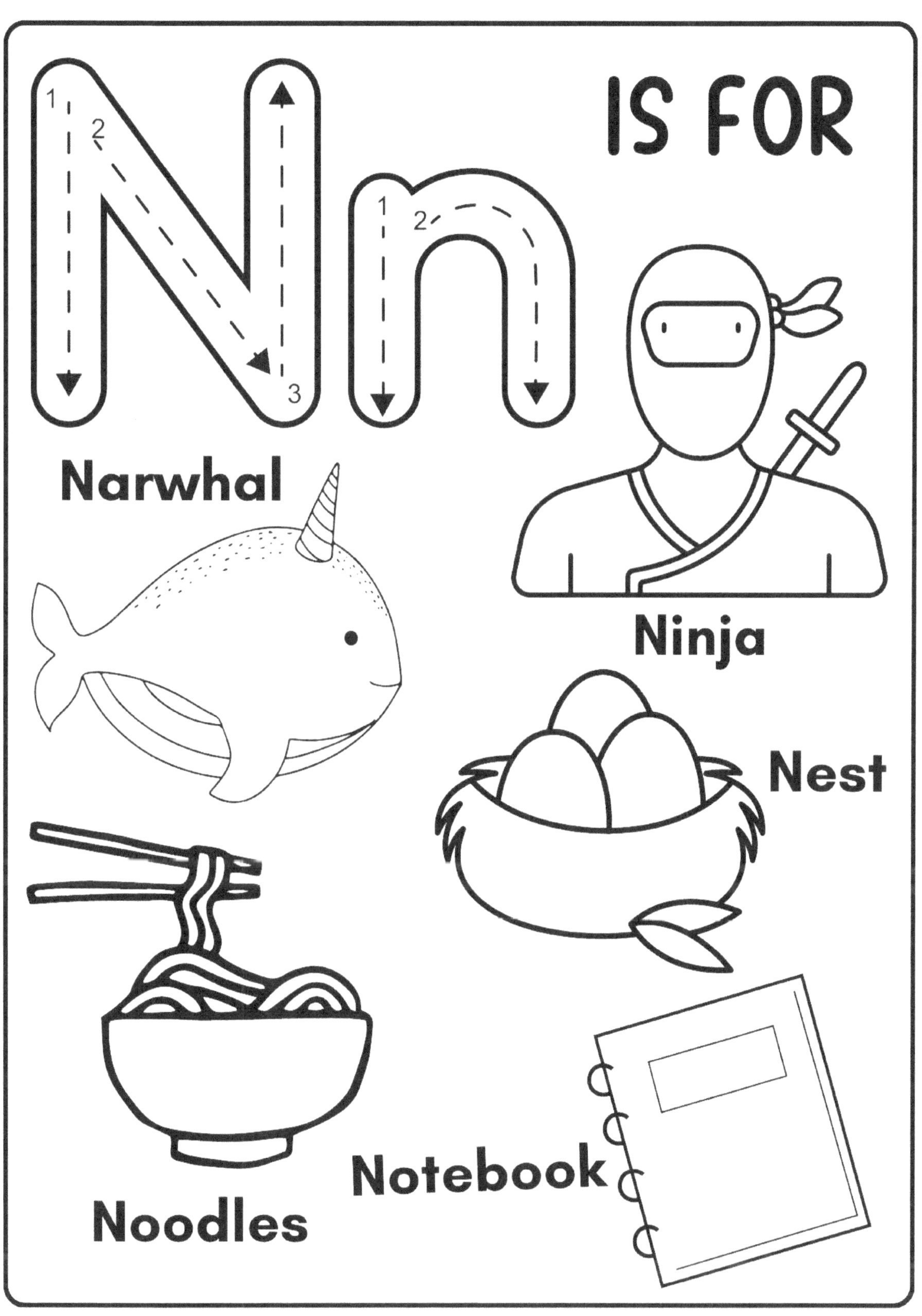

IS FOR
Narwhal
Ninja
Nest
Noodles
Notebook

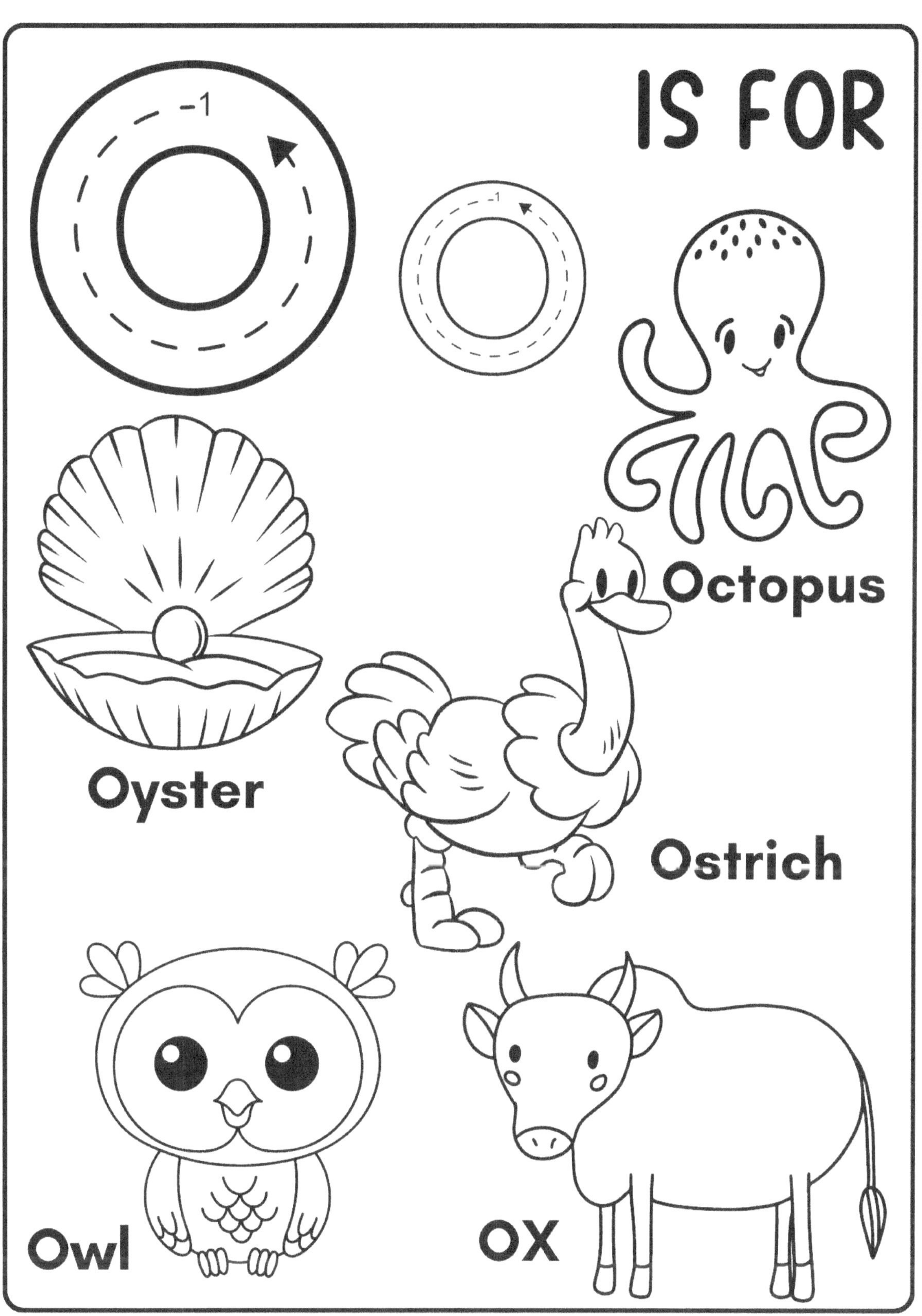

IS FOR
Octopus
Oyster
Ostrich
Owl
OX

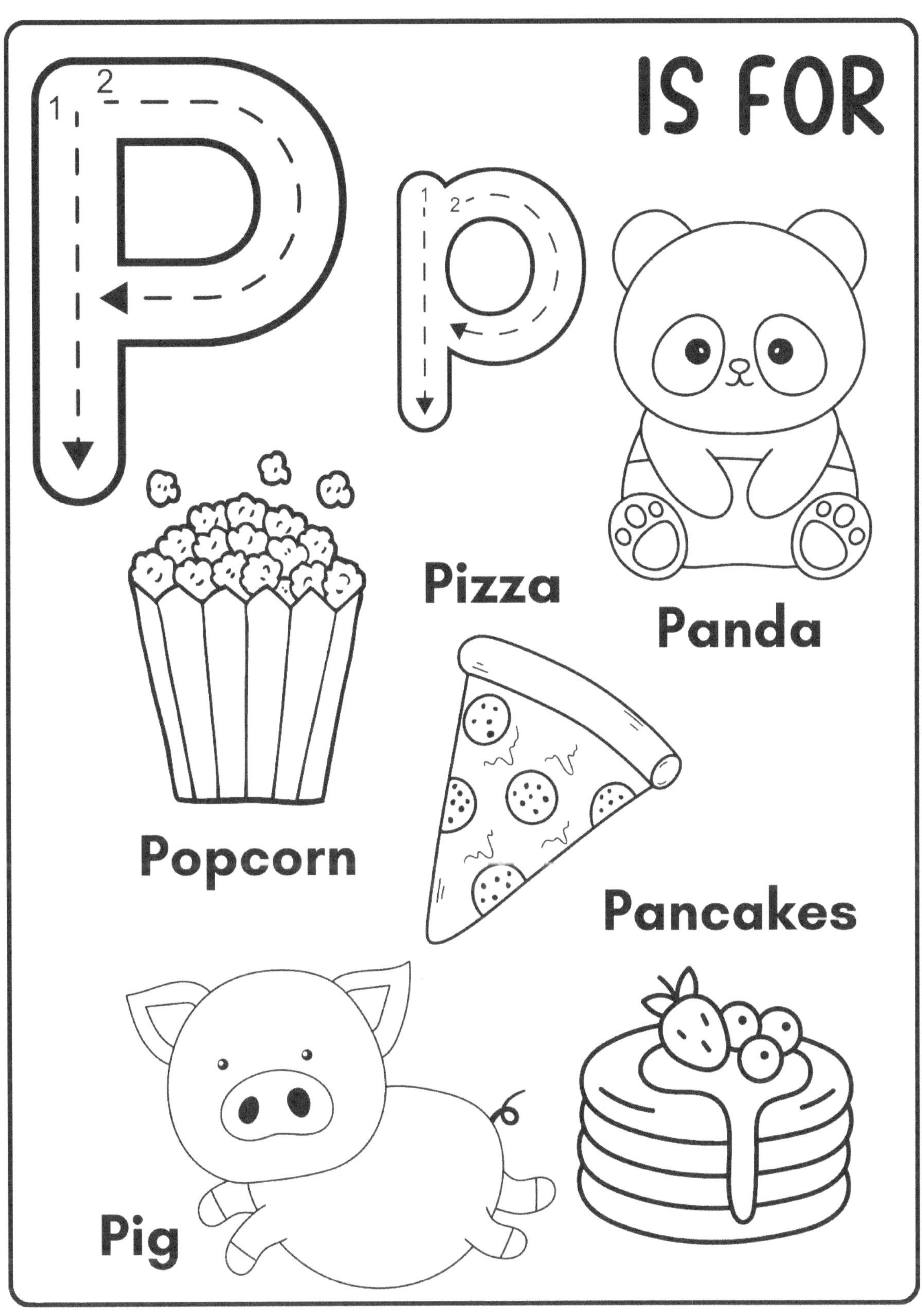

P
p
IS FOR
Popcorn
Pizza
Panda
Pancakes
Pig

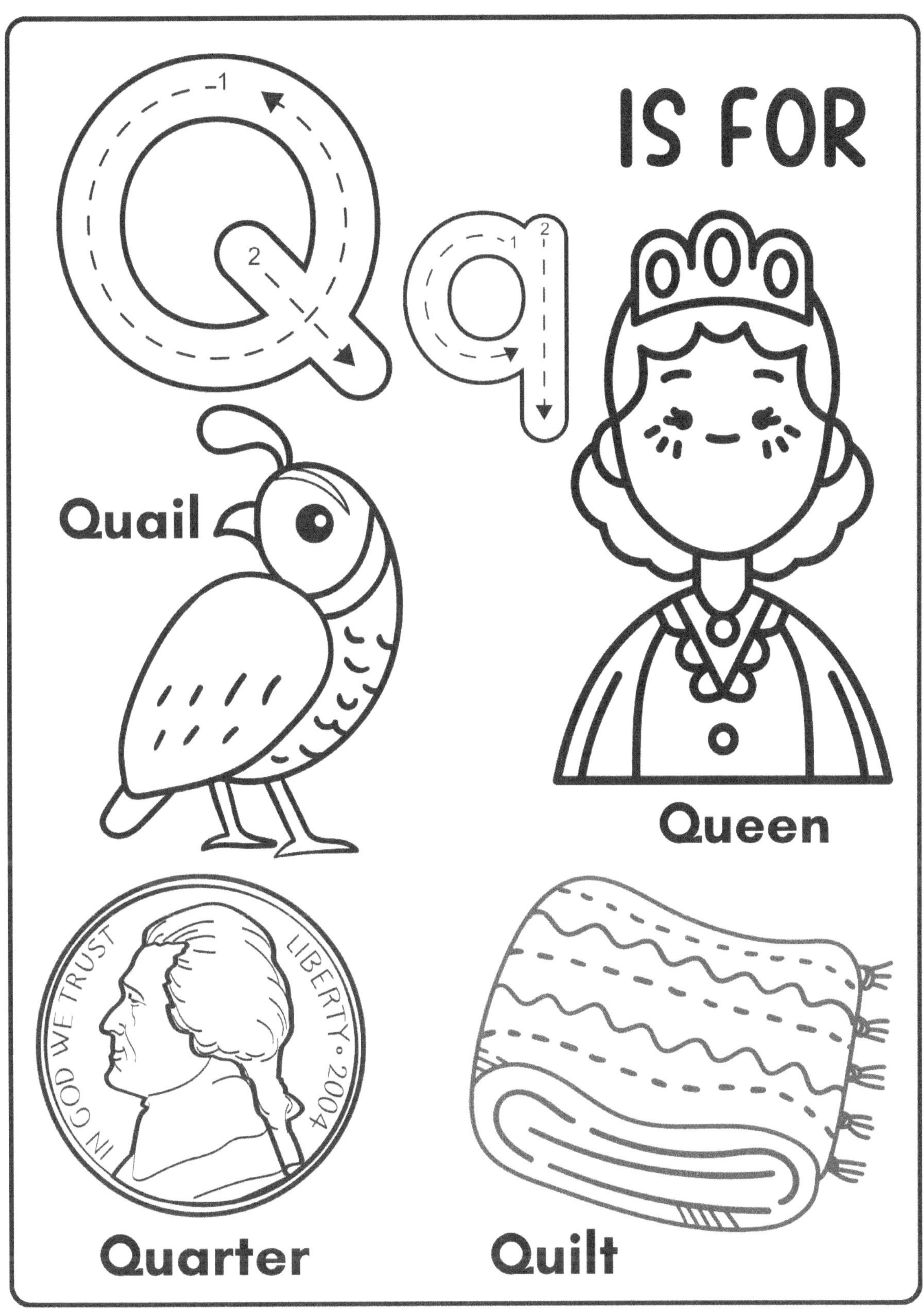

Q q
IS FOR
Quail
Queen
Quarter
Quilt
IN GOD WE TRUST
LIBERTY
2004

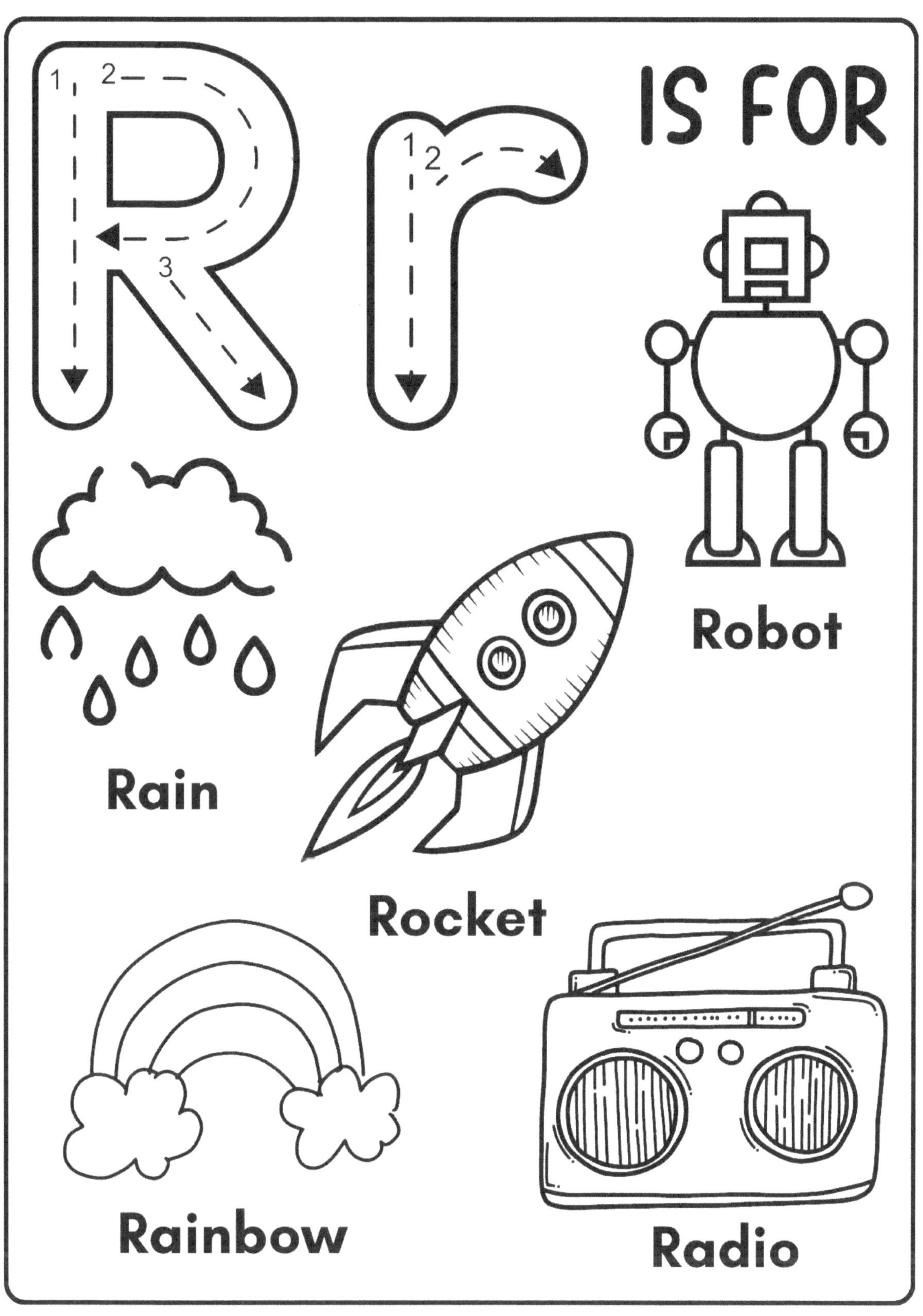

R r
IS FOR
1 2
1 2
3
Robot
Rain
Rocket
Rainbow
Radio

S s   IS FOR

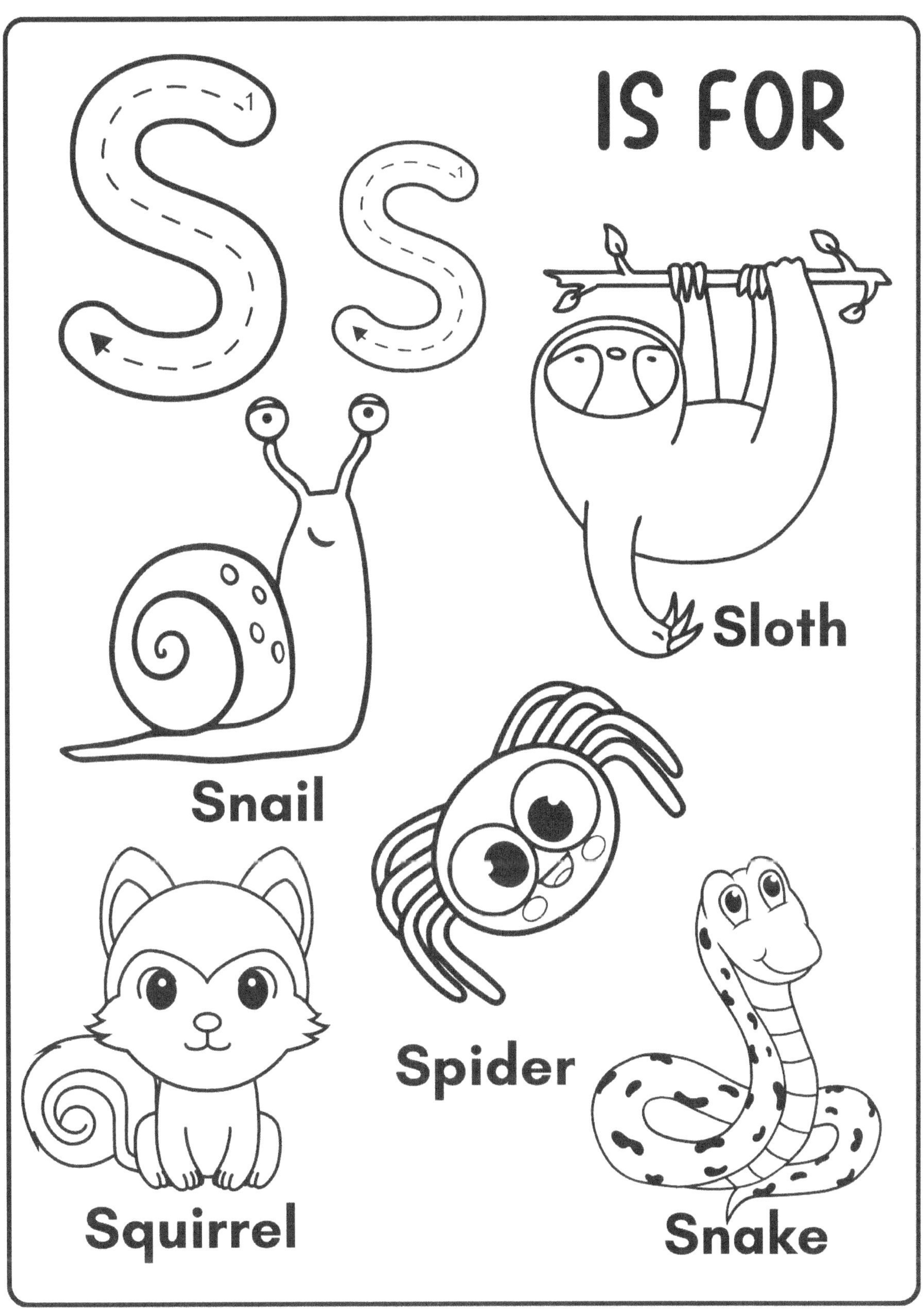

T IS FOR

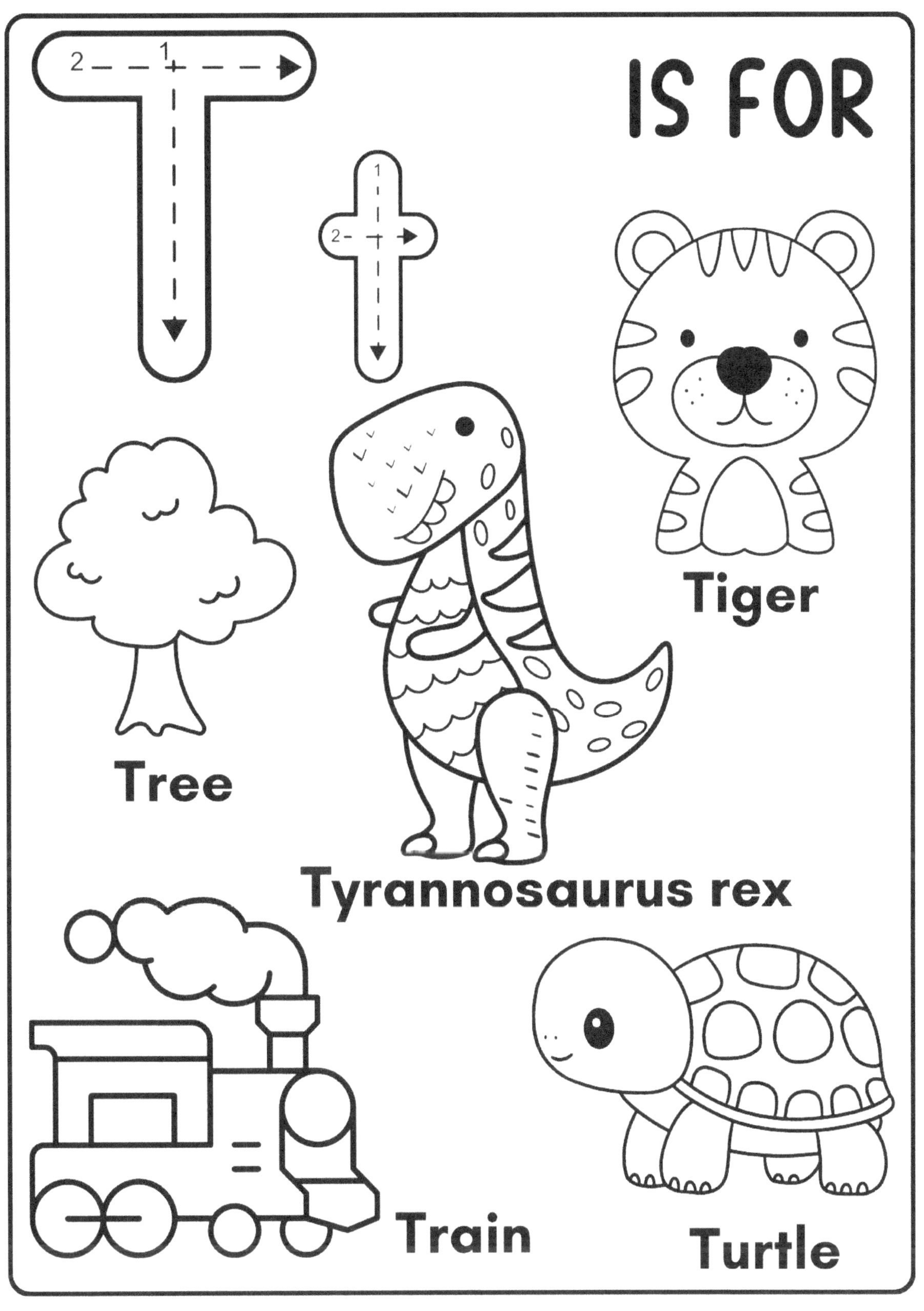

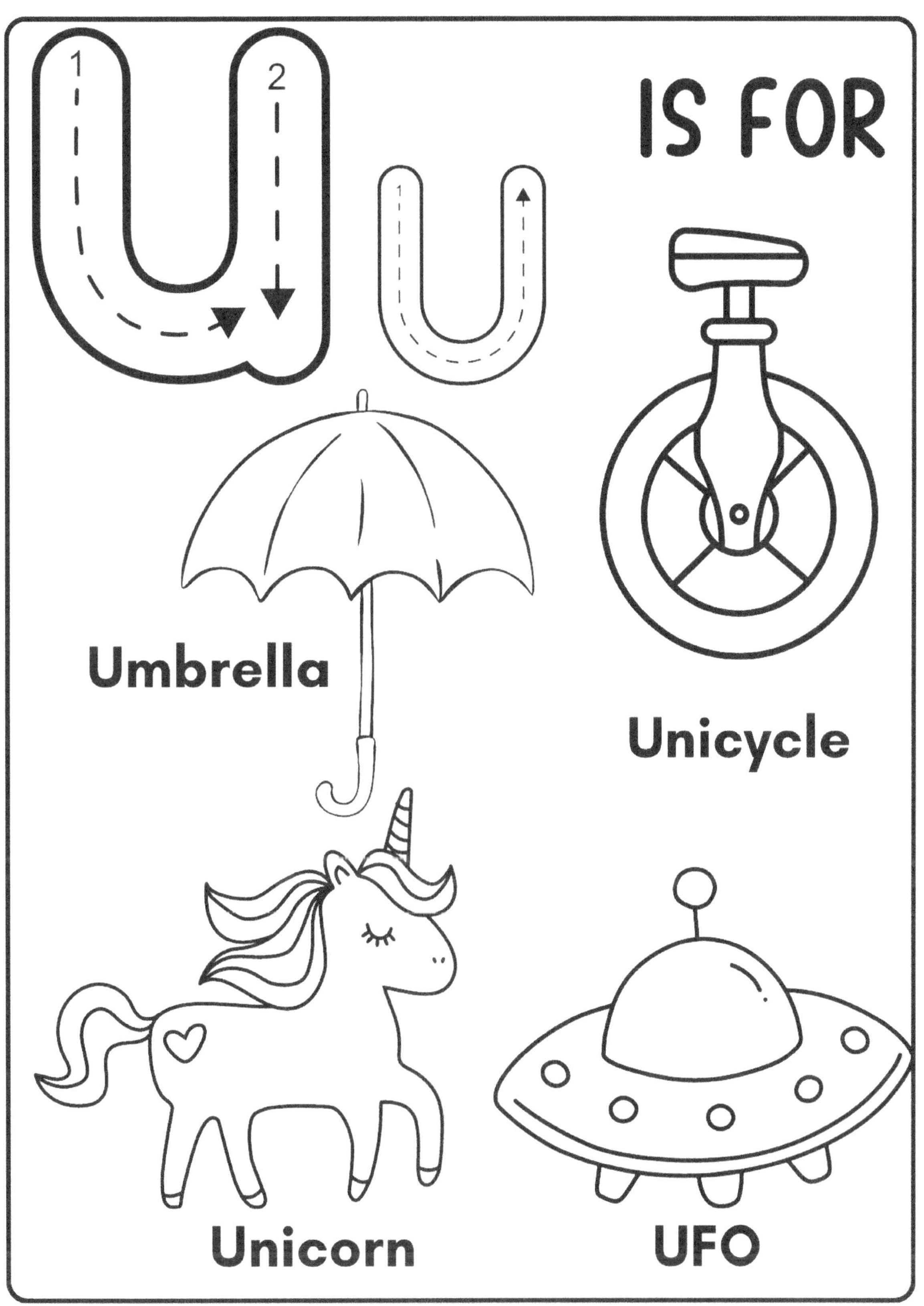

IS FOR
Umbrella
Unicycle
Unicorn
UFO

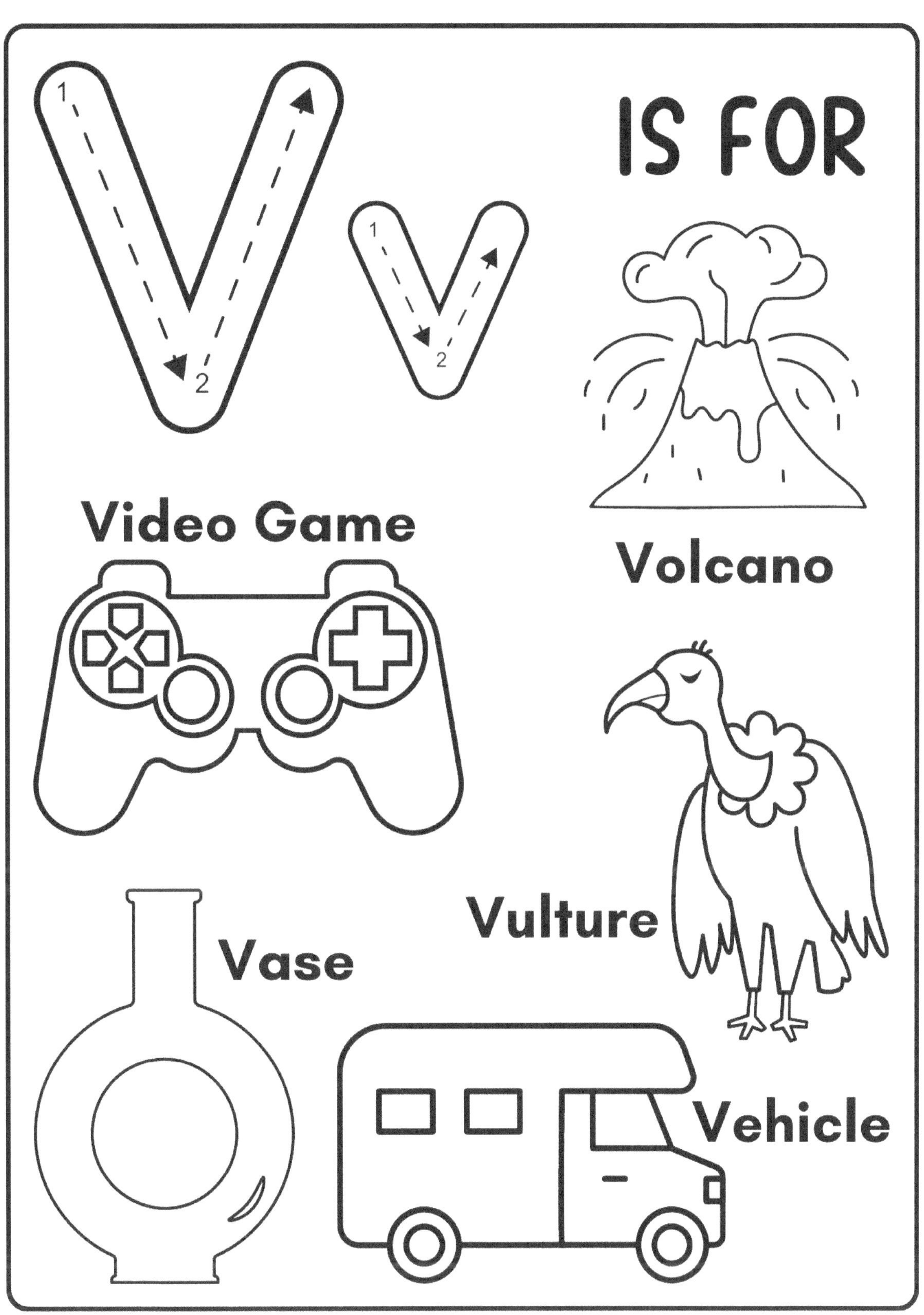

IS FOR
Video Game
Volcano
Vulture
Vase
Vehicle

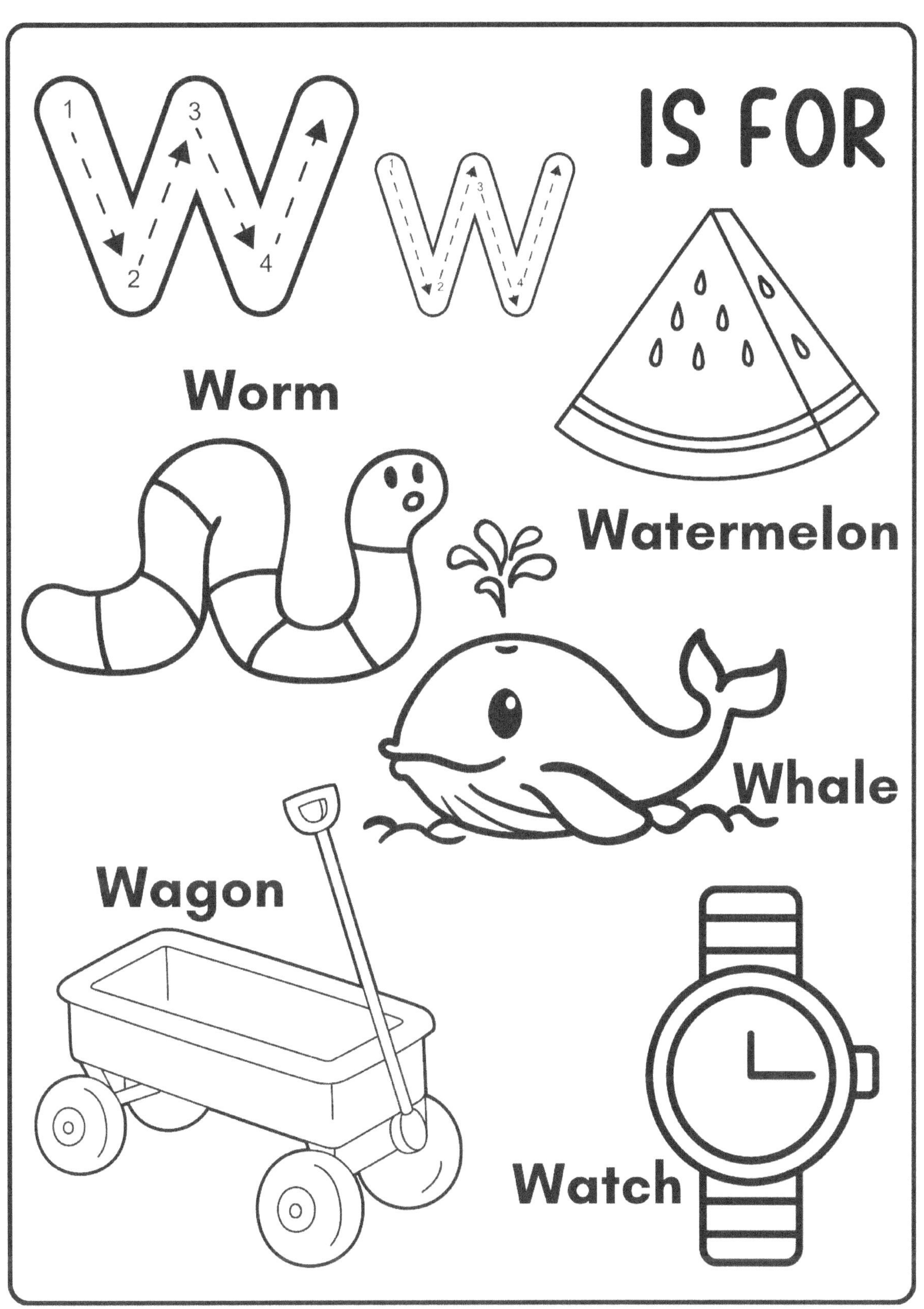
IS FOR
Worm
Watermelon
Whale
Wagon
Watch

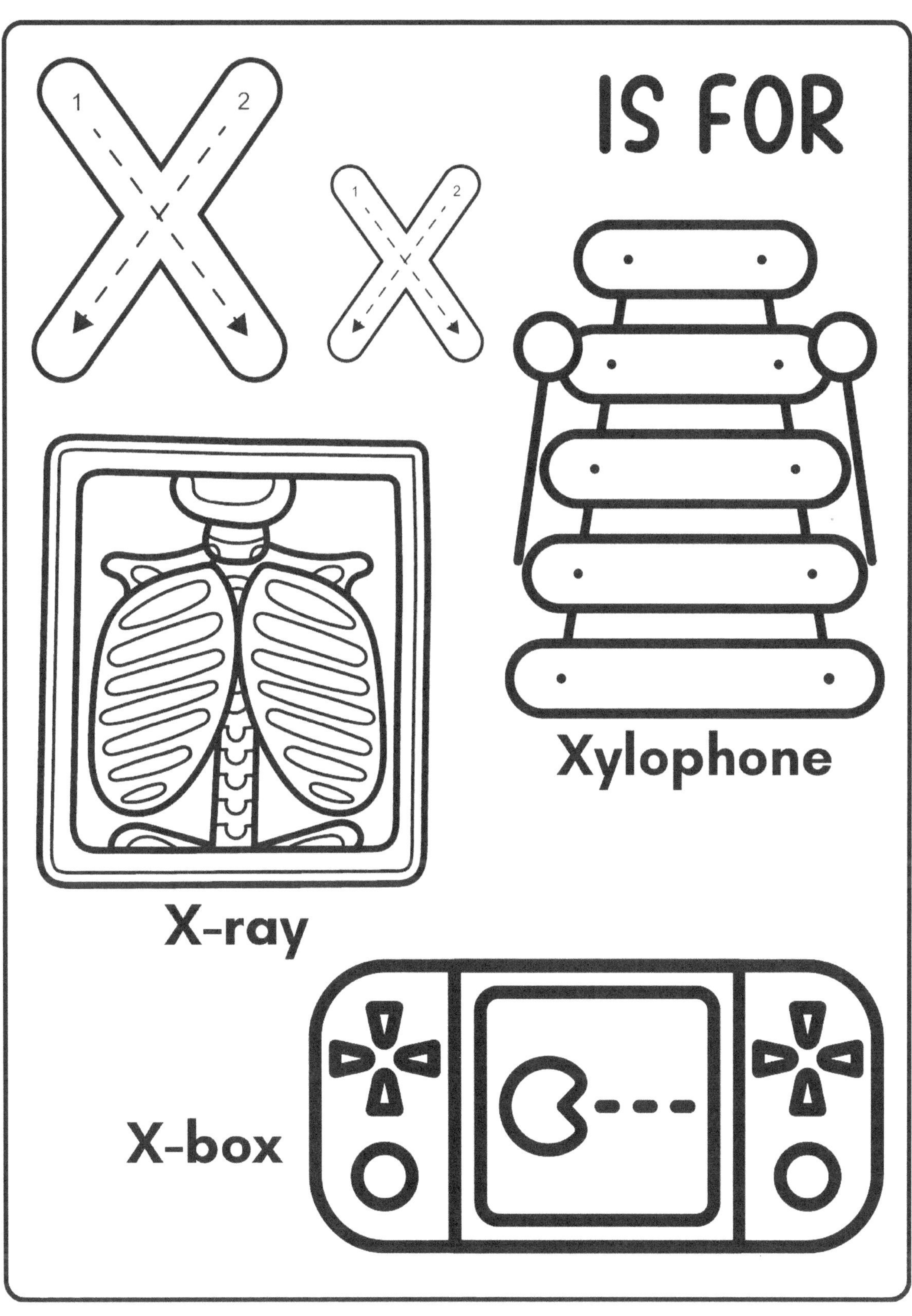

IS FOR
Xylophone
X-ray
X-box

Y y

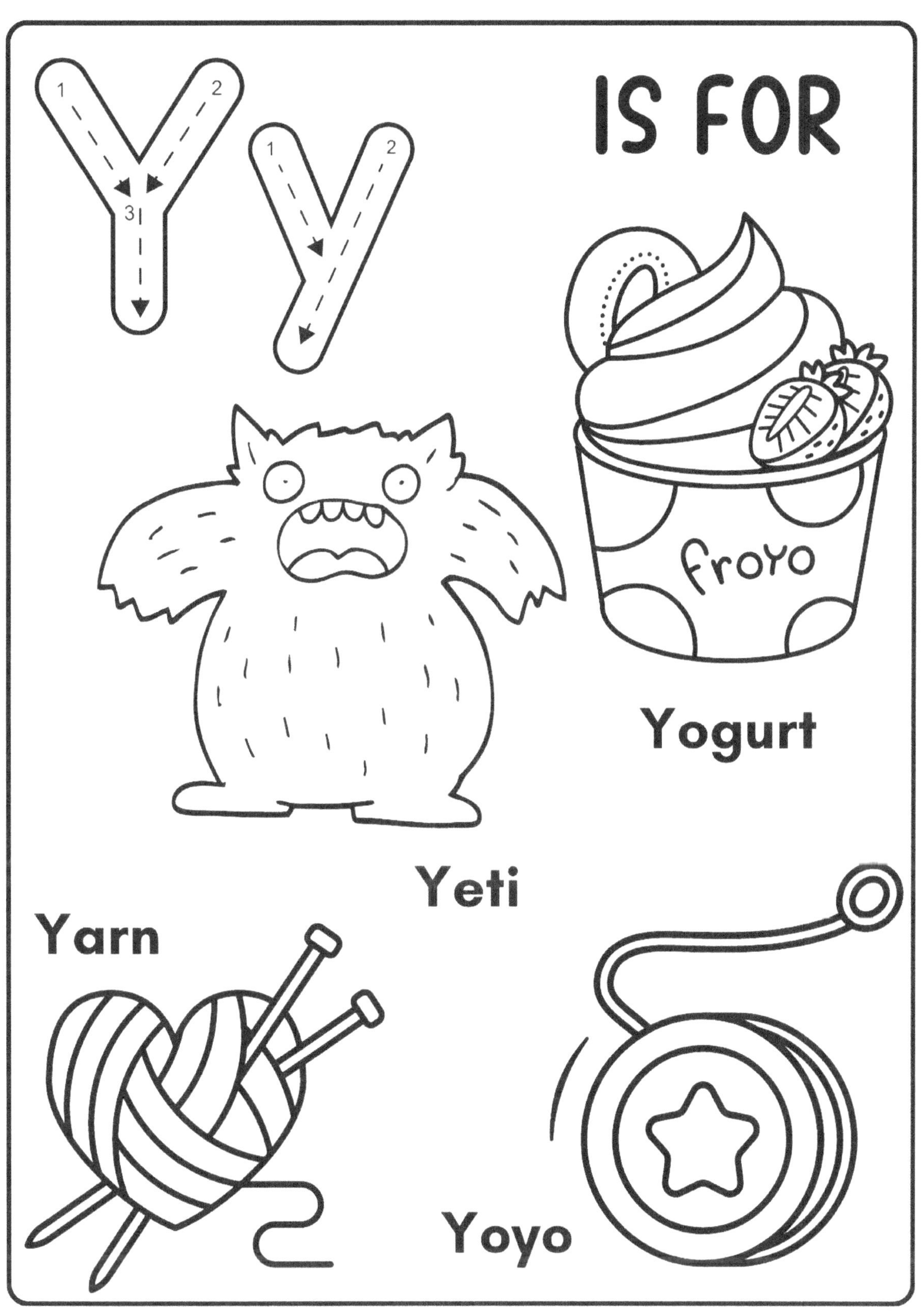

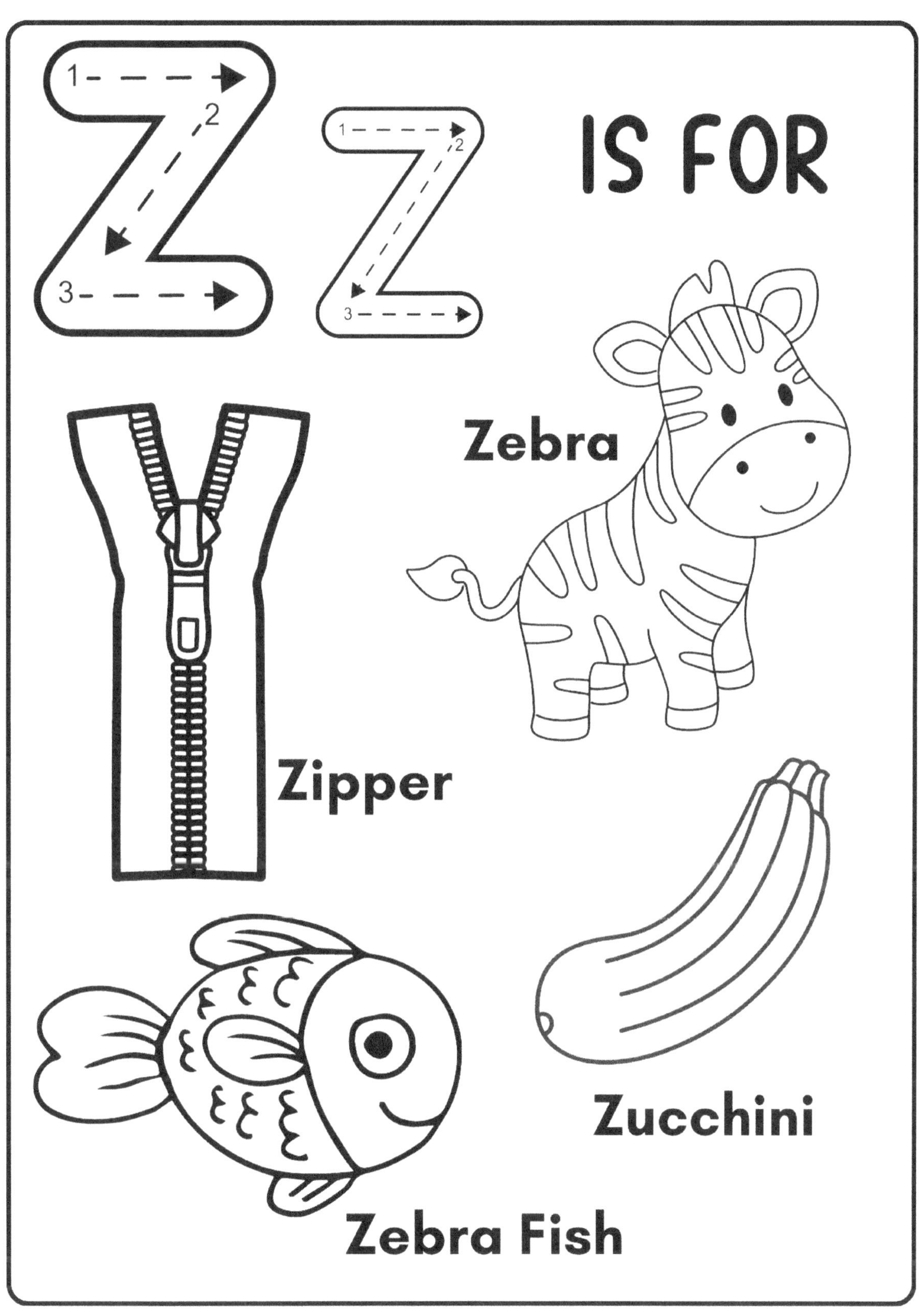

Z z IS FOR
Zebra
Zipper
Zucchini
Zebra Fish